Courtesy of Neues Museum, Berlin, Germany

Photograph of the bust of Nefertiti, wife of an Egyptian pharaoh – one of the most famous Egyptian art masterpieces – crafted in 1345 BC

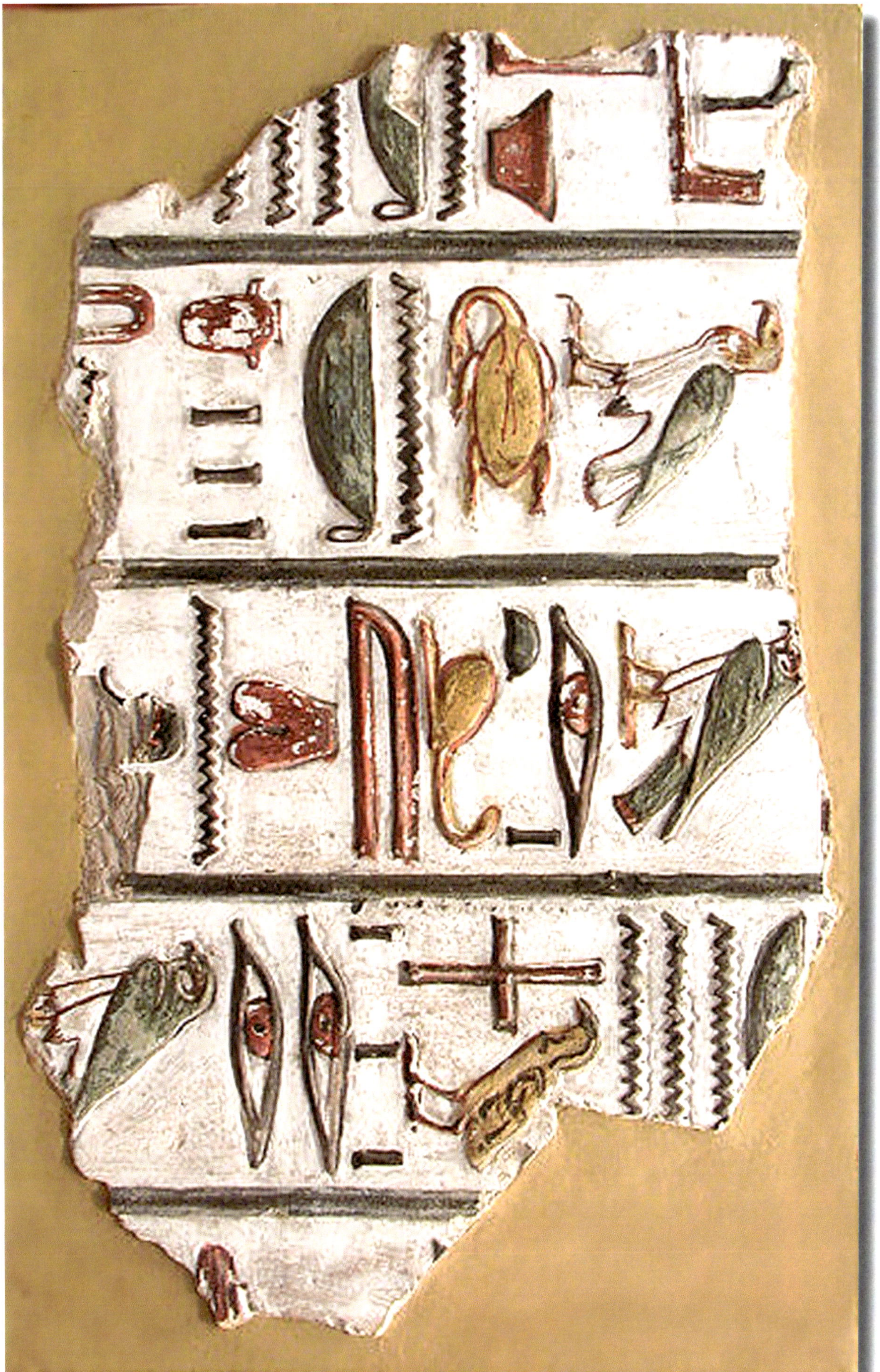

Courtesy of Jon Bodsworth

Photograph of hieroglyphs from the tomb of Pharaoh Seti I – 13th century BC

Courtesy of The Yorck Project

Painting of farmer plowing with a yoke of horned cattle – painting from the burial chamber of Sennedjem – circa 1200 BC

Courtesy of *The British Museum Book of Ancient Egypt*

Vignette from the Book of the Dead of Penmaat – a priest of Amun, Penmaat is shown burning incense and displaying the shaved head required for priestly purity – circa 950 BC

Courtesy of Wikimedia Commons

Farming scenes from a tomb showing workers plowing the fields, harvesting crops, and threshing grain – copy of a 15th century BC picture

Courtesy of Wellcome Images

Lithograph of the decorated pillars of the temple at Karnac, Thebes, Egypt – 1846

Courtesy of Library of Congress

Photograph of the Sphinx and Cheops Pyramid – 1901

Courtesy of Harry Burton

Photograph showing excavation of Tutankhamun's tomb in the Valley of the Kings – 1922

Courtesy of *The New York Times*

Photograph of archaeologist Howard Carter opening the innermost shrine of King Tutankhamun's tomb near Luxor, Egypt – 1922

Courtesy of NASA

Satellite image of the Nile River and delta as seen from space – 2003

Photograph of mummy from the Egyptian collection at the British Museum in London, England – photo taken 2004

Courtesy of Guillaume Blanchard (CC BY-SA 1.0)

Photograph of a typical Naqada II jar (from the Predynastic Period) decorated with gazelles – photo taken 2004

Courtesy of Jeff Dahl (CC BY-SA 3.0)

Photograph of slab showing ancient Egyptian medical instruments, including bone saws, suction cups, knives and scalpels, retractors, scales, lances, chisels and dental tools – photo taken 2005

Photograph of the Giza pyramids – 2006

Courtesy of Steve F-E-Cameron, Creative Commons

Photograph of Temple of Horus at Edfu – photo taken 2006

Courtesy of Carole Raddato (CC BY-SA 2.0)

Photograph of statue of Egyptian goddess Bastet – the ancient Egyptians revered cats – photo taken 2012

Photograph of tile depicting the Eye of Horus, ancient Egyptian symbol of protection, royal power and good health – photo taken 2012

Courtesy of Serge Haviani (CC BY-SA 3.0)

Photograph of troop of funerary servant figurines (ushabtis) in ancient Egyptian tomb – photo taken 2013

Photograph of the entrance to the Luxor Temple – constructed approximately 1400 BCE – photo taken 2015

ANCIENT EGYPT

Primary Sources

Historical Documents • Maps • Photographs • Political Cartoons

INCLUDES 20 PRIMARY SOURCE DOCUMENTS:

- Photograph of the bust of Nefertiti, wife of an Egyptian pharaoh – one of the most famous Egyptian art masterpieces – crafted in 1345 BC
- Photograph of hieroglyphs from the tomb of Pharaoh Seti I – 13th century BC
- Painting of farmer plowing with a yoke of horned cattle – painting from the burial chamber of Sennedjem – circa 1200 BC
- Vignette from the Book of the Dead of Penmaat – a priest of Amun, Penmaat is shown burning incense and displaying the shaved head required for priestly purity – circa 950 BC
- Farming scenes from a tomb showing workers plowing the fields, harvesting crops, and threshing grain – copy of a 15th century BC picture
- Lithograph of the decorated pillars of the temple at Karnac, Thebes, Egypt – 1846
- Photograph of the Sphinx and Cheops Pyramid – 1901
- Photograph showing excavation of Tutankhamun's tomb in the Valley of the Kings – 1922
- Photograph of archaeologist Howard Carter opening the innermost shrine of King Tutankhamun's tomb near Luxor, Egypt – 1922\
- Photograph of mummy from the Egyptian collection at the British Museum in London, England – photo taken 2004
- Photograph of a typical Naqada II jar (from the Predynastic Period) decorated with gazelles – photo taken 2004
- Photograph of slab showing ancient Egyptian medical instruments, including bone saws, suction cups, knives and scalpels, retractors, scales, lances, chisels and dental tools – photo taken 2005
- Photograph of the Giza pyramids – 2006
- Photograph of Temple of Horus at Edfu – photo taken 2006
- Slab showing two figures of the Egyptian god Hapi tying papyrus and reed plants in the *sema tawy* symbol for the unification of Upper and Lower Egypt – photo taken 2009
- Photograph of statue of Egyptian goddess Bastet – the ancient Egyptians revered cats – photo taken 2012
- Photograph of tile depicting the Eye of Horus, ancient Egyptian symbol of protection, royal power and good health – photo taken 2012
- Photograph of troop of funerary servant figurines (ushabtis) in ancient Egyptian tomb – photo taken 2013
- Photograph of the entrance to the Luxor Temple – constructed approximately 1400 BCE – photo taken 2015

Perfect for Gallery Walks & Literature Circles!

Build Higher-Order Thinking Skills:

- Analysis
- Critical Thinking
- Point of View
- Compare and Contrast
- Order of Events
- & Much More!

FREE 15-page Online Teacher's Guide! www.gallopade.com/pstg

GALLOPADE

www.gallopade.com
Printed in Peachtree City, GA

ISBN-13: 978-0-635-12597-2 $17.99
51799
9 780635 125972 7 10430 12458 9

STANDARDS-BASED LEARNING & FUN!

THE ROARING TWENTIES
AMERICAN CULTURE IN THE 1920s
Primary Sources

20 Primary Sources!
We dug through the archives so you don't have to!

ACADEMICS' CHOICE™ SMART BOOK AWARD WINNER

TEACH IT TODAY! CORE RESOURCE™

by Carole Marsh

Courtesy of Library of Congress

Photograph of young immigrants at Ellis Island, New York – circa 1915-1920

Courtesy of Library of Congress

Political cartoon depicting the women's suffrage movement in the United States – the 19th Amendment was passed in 1920, giving women the right to vote – 1917

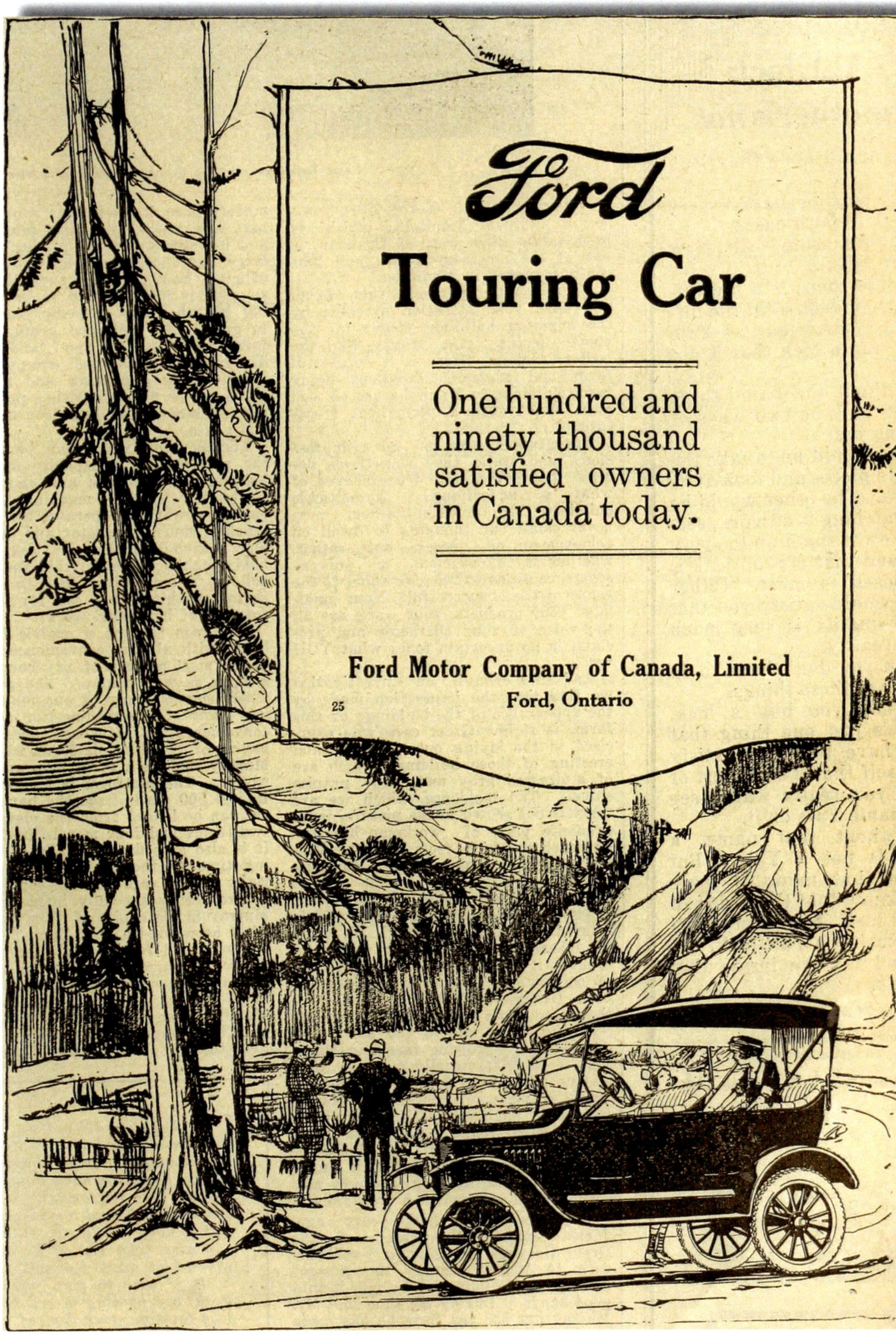

Courtesy of University of Toronto

Copy of advertisement for a Ford touring car in *Farmers Magazine* – 1920

Courtesy of Library of Congress

U.S. presidential candidates Warren G. Harding and James M. Cox discuss Babe Ruth's record-breaking home run tally – 1920

Courtesy of Library of Congress

Photograph of Babe Ruth – 1920

Photograph of major league baseball superstar Babe Ruth and political cartoon depicting national interest in his accomplishments

Courtesy of Library of Congress

Newspaper advertisement for the Kelvinator refrigerator – electric refrigerators began to replace ice boxes in the early 1900s – ad published 1920

Courtesy of Wikimedia Commons

Self-portrait by Walt Disney used on his business envelopes as he began his career as a cartoonist – 1921

Courtesy of Library of Congress

Photograph of New York City police commissioner watching agents pour liquor into a sewer after a raid during Prohibition – 1921

Courtesy of Indiana University

Cover page for song "I'm Just Wild About Harry" from the Broadway show *Shuffle Along*– first financially successful Broadway play with African American writers and an all-African American cast – 1921

Courtesy of Saturday Evening Post

Saturday Evening Post magazine cover titled "The Flapper" – 1922

Courtesy of Library of Congress

Photograph of Ford Motor Company assembly line – Henry Ford's assembly line concept revolutionized the manufacturing industry – 1923

Courtesy of Library of Congress

Photograph of President Calvin Coolidge throwing out a baseball at a major league baseball game – Calvin Coolidge served as the 30th U.S. president from 1923 to 1929 – photo taken 1924

Courtesy of Library of Congress

Photograph of women tuning a radio – listening to radio in the 1920s was an exciting new form of entertainment – circa 1925

Mother to Son

by Langston Hughes

Well, son, I'll tell you:
Life for me ain't been no crystal stair.
It's had tacks in it,
And splinters,
And boards torn up,
And places with no carpet on the floor—
Bare.
But all the time
I'se been a-climbin' on,
And reachin' landin's,
And turnin' corners,
And sometimes goin' in the dark
Where there ain't been no light.
So boy, don't you turn back.
Don't you set down on the steps
'Cause you finds it's kinder hard.
Don't you fall now—
For I'se still goin', honey,
I'se still climbin',
And life for me ain't been no crystal stair.

Courtesy of The Weary Blues by Langston Hughes, copyright 1926

Poem titled "Mother to Son" by Langston Hughes

Courtesy of Library of Congress

Photograph of Langston Hughes – 1942

Photograph of Langston Hughes and the words to his poem "Mother to Son" – Hughes was a leader of the Harlem Renaissance in New York City

Courtesy of Wikimedia Commons

Entertainer Josephine Baker performs the "Charleston," a popular dance during the Roaring 20s – 1926

Courtesy of Library of Congress

Photograph of Charles Lindbergh in front of his airplane, *Spirit of St. Louis*– Lindbergh is famous for completing the first transatlantic flight – 1927

Courtesy of Wikimedia Commons

Copy of movie poster for *The Jazz Singer* – its release signaled the growth of sound films and ended the silent film era – 1927

Courtesy of Library of Congress

Photograph of crowd outside the New York Stock Exchange after the stock market crash – 1929

Courtesy of Wikimedia Commons

Photograph of a workman on the framework of the Empire State Building – builders competed to build the tallest skyscraper in New York City in the 1920s – photo taken 1930

Courtesy of Library of Congress

Photograph of jazz musician Louis Armstrong – 1952